Dedicated to:
Kate, Zach, Will, Lizzie, Nathan, Jack, Jeremiah, Micah, Isaiah,
Chloe, Naomi, Ben, Elijah,
to the tenth generation.

This book is given to

....

with love from

....

If you are a mother or grandmother or need a baby gift, this book is for you! Beautifully illustrated, it shares God's truth about marriage in a winsome way while dealing with tough issues. It's a great starting place for young children.

SUSAN ALEXANDER YATES

Author of *And Then I Had Kids* and *Risky Faith*

There are many reasons I admire Jani Ortlund. One of those reasons is the example she sets as a wise teacher and cultivator of the next generation. This book is a perfect example of that leadership. Many would assume that marriage is something people need to start thinking about sometime in their twenties or thirties. God designed marriage though to teach us about him. That's true not only for those who are now married but even for those who someday will be. This book introduces children to the beauty of God's picture of the gospel in marriage and family in a way that children can understand and love.

RUSSELL MOORE

Theologian, Christianity Today Magazine

Full of Jani's characteristic wisdom, this little book will be a great help to any parent who cares about truly nurturing and shaping their child's heart. Doing so in the things that really matter and in a day when it matters more and more.

JOHN AND JOAN KIRKPATRICK

Pastor of Portrush Presbyterian Church, Portrush, Northern Ireland

Leave it to Jani Ortlund to write a much-needed children's book about marriage! In her usual clear yet winsome way, she covers a host of important topics in this short book and backs them all up with Scripture. The message of the gospel is woven throughout as she carefully discusses marriage, divorce and same sex marriage in a way that young readers will understand. What a welcome work this will be for parents seeking to train their children that God's way is indeed always best.

MARY K. MOHLER

Director, Seminary Wives Institute, The Southern Baptist Theological Seminary, Louisville, Kentucky

A Child's FIRST Book About MARRIAGE

God's Way is Always Best

Jani Ortlund
Illustrated by Angelo Ruta

You probably know a lot of people who are married—your mom and dad, your grandparents, some of your aunts and uncles, maybe your neighbor or your teacher or your pastor. A lot of people get married. Have you ever wondered why? Did you ever wonder why your dad and mom married each other? Who invented this thing called marriage?

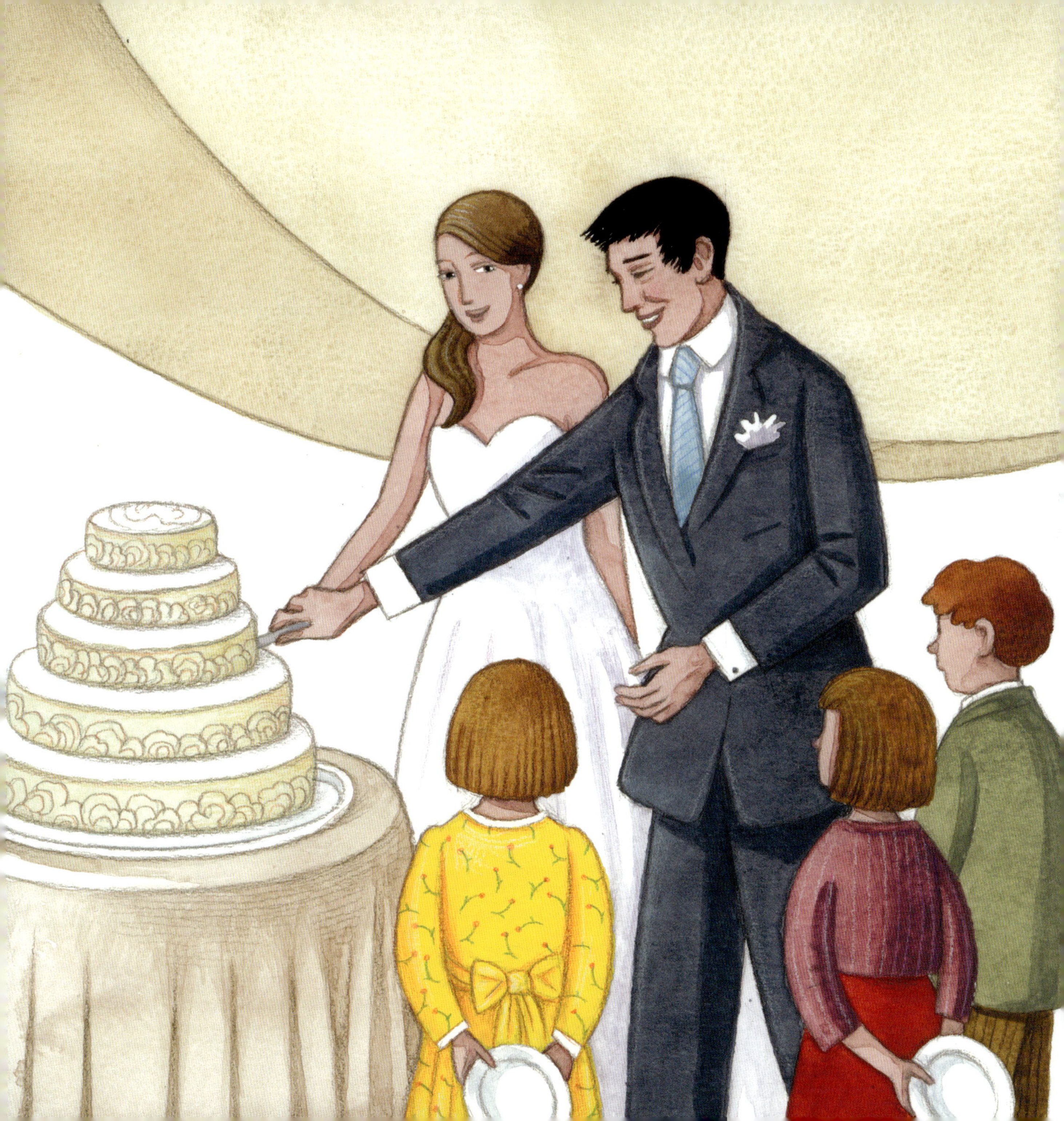

*M*arriage has been around for a long time. It's older than your parents or grandparents. It's older than the Statue of Liberty or the Great Wall of China. It's even older than the ancient pyramids of Egypt.

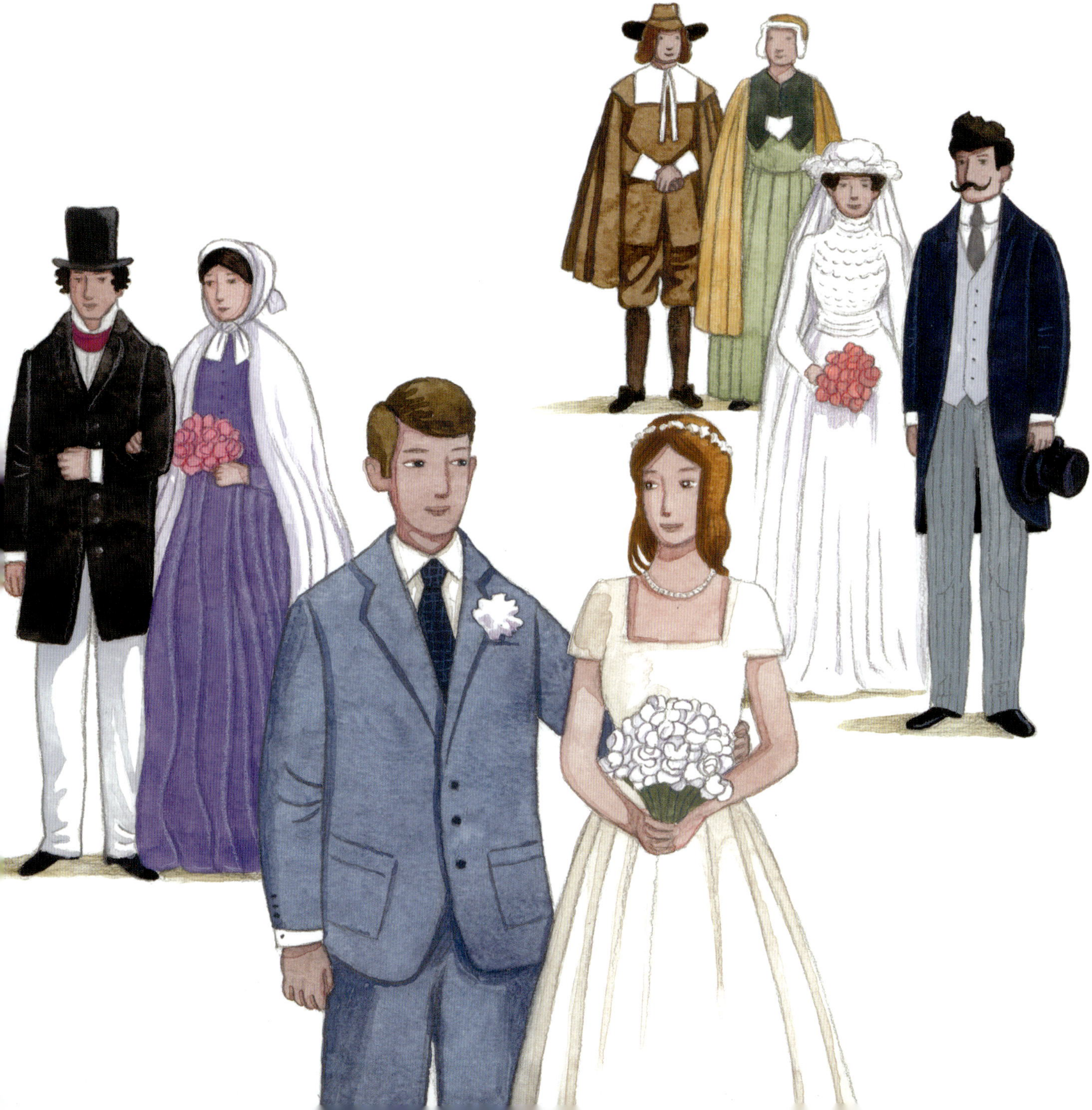

Marriage began all the way back in the perfect Garden of Eden. That's where God made the very first man and the very first woman, and that's where God created marriage.

Even in this beautiful garden with all the animals to play with, and with God to keep Adam company, there was still something missing. God knew that Adam needed someone strong and lovely and smart and kind. He needed someone like him but also different from him. God knew that Adam needed a wife!

God made the first woman, Eve, out of Adam's body. She was so special that God formed her in a different way than anything else He had ever made! And after God made her, He brought her to Adam, like the father of the bride in the very first wedding in the whole world (Genesis 2:20-22).

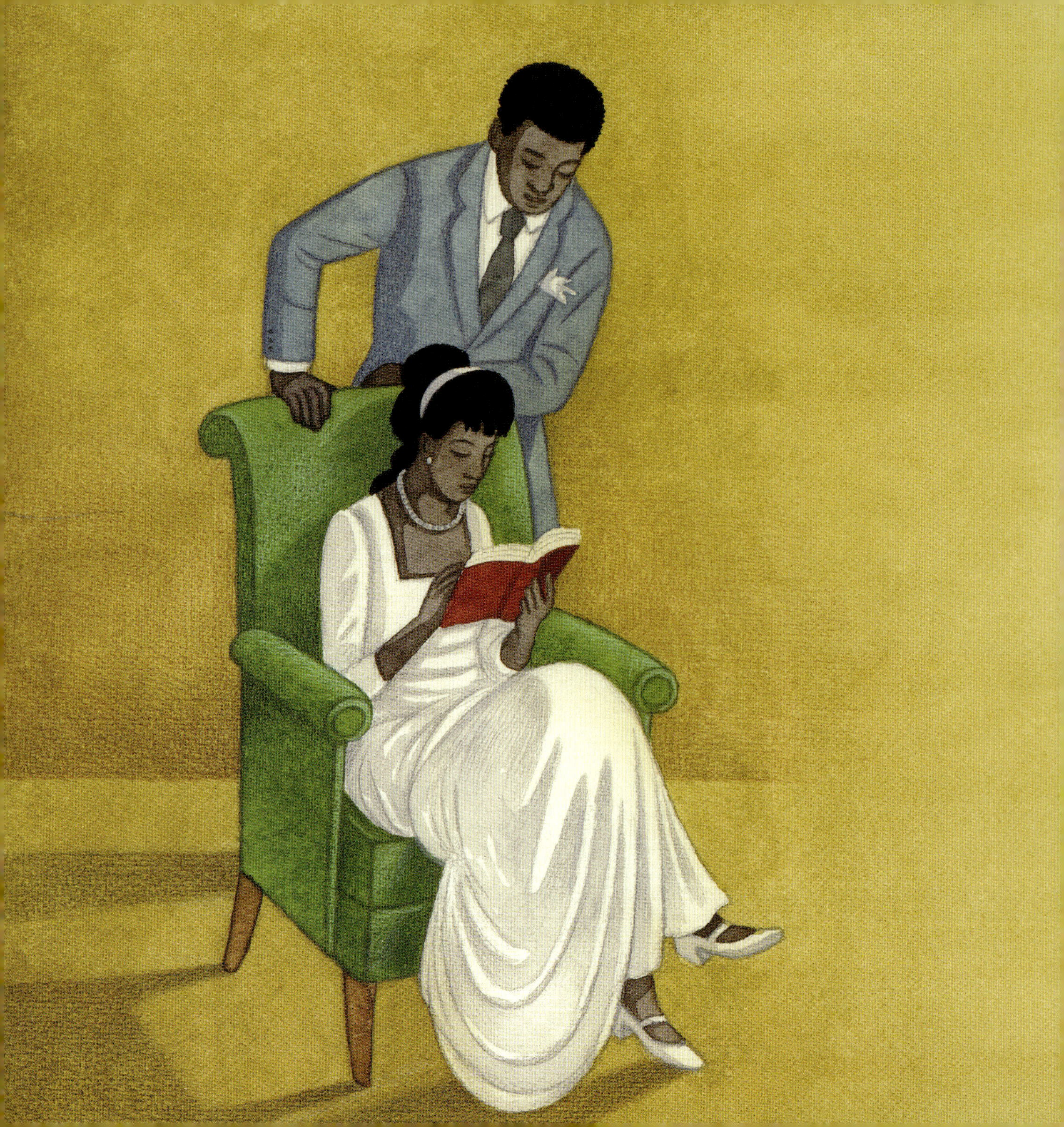

Ever since that first wedding, people have been getting married. Just like everything that comes from the heart of God, marriage is beautiful and good. God tells us that marriage is one man and one woman giving all of themselves to each other for their whole lives (Matthew 19:4-6; Ephesians 5:31-33).

When a man and a woman marry, God doesn't just see two "me's" anymore. He sees one "us"!

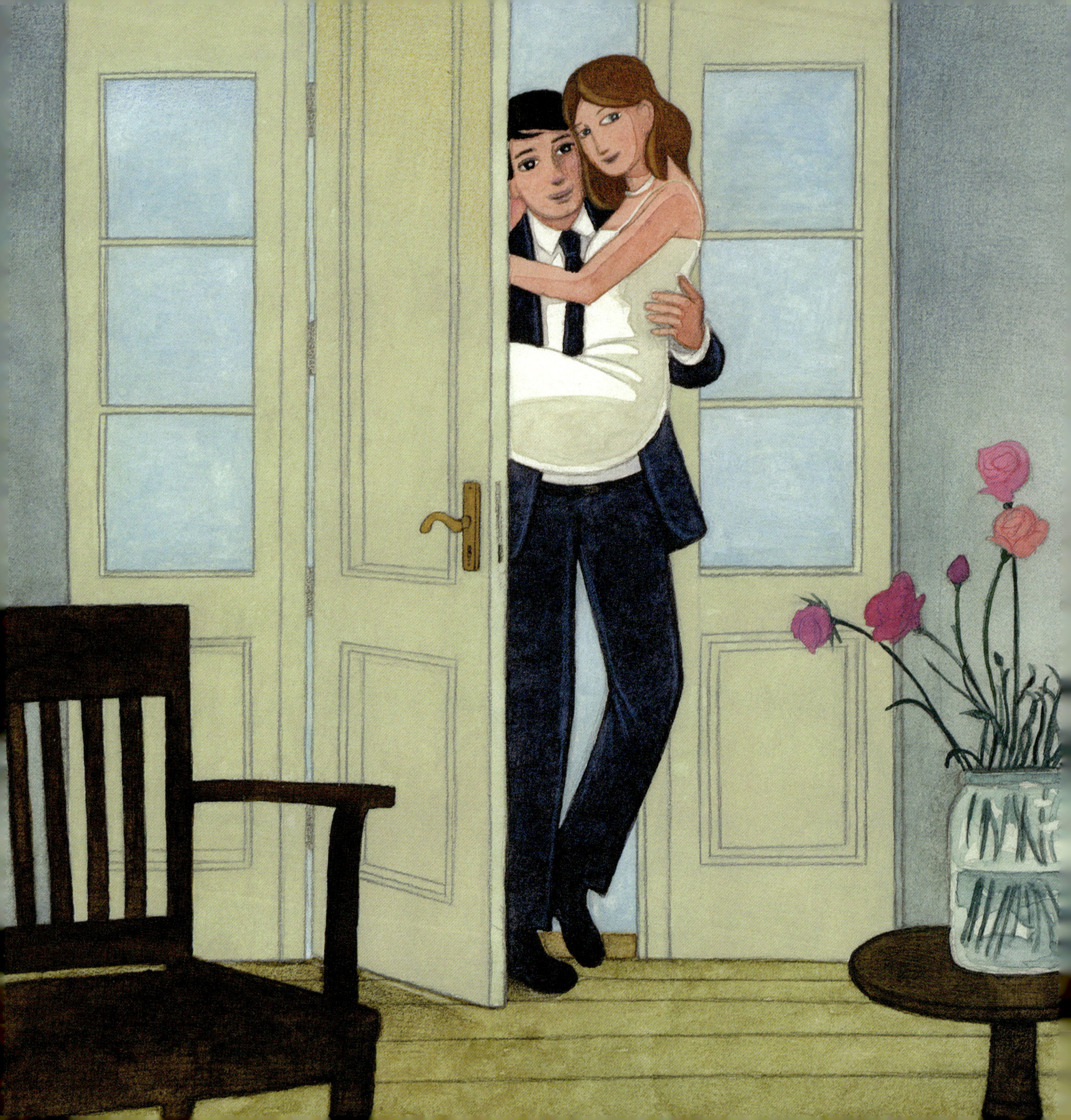

Jesus says that when a man and woman get married, God joins them together in the most special of all relationships here on earth. God looks at the two of them as one, and no one should ever separate them (Mark 10:6-9).

When a man and a woman marry, they share their hearts, their thoughts, even their bodies! (Do you ever see your mom and dad kiss? Married people do that!) They share the same name, the same money, the same house—even the same bed!

𝒜 husband and wife become more special to each other than to anyone else in the whole world. When one is sad, there is someone who cares. When one needs advice, there is someone to ask. When one gets hurt, there is someone to help. When one loses, they stick together, and when one wins, they both cheer!

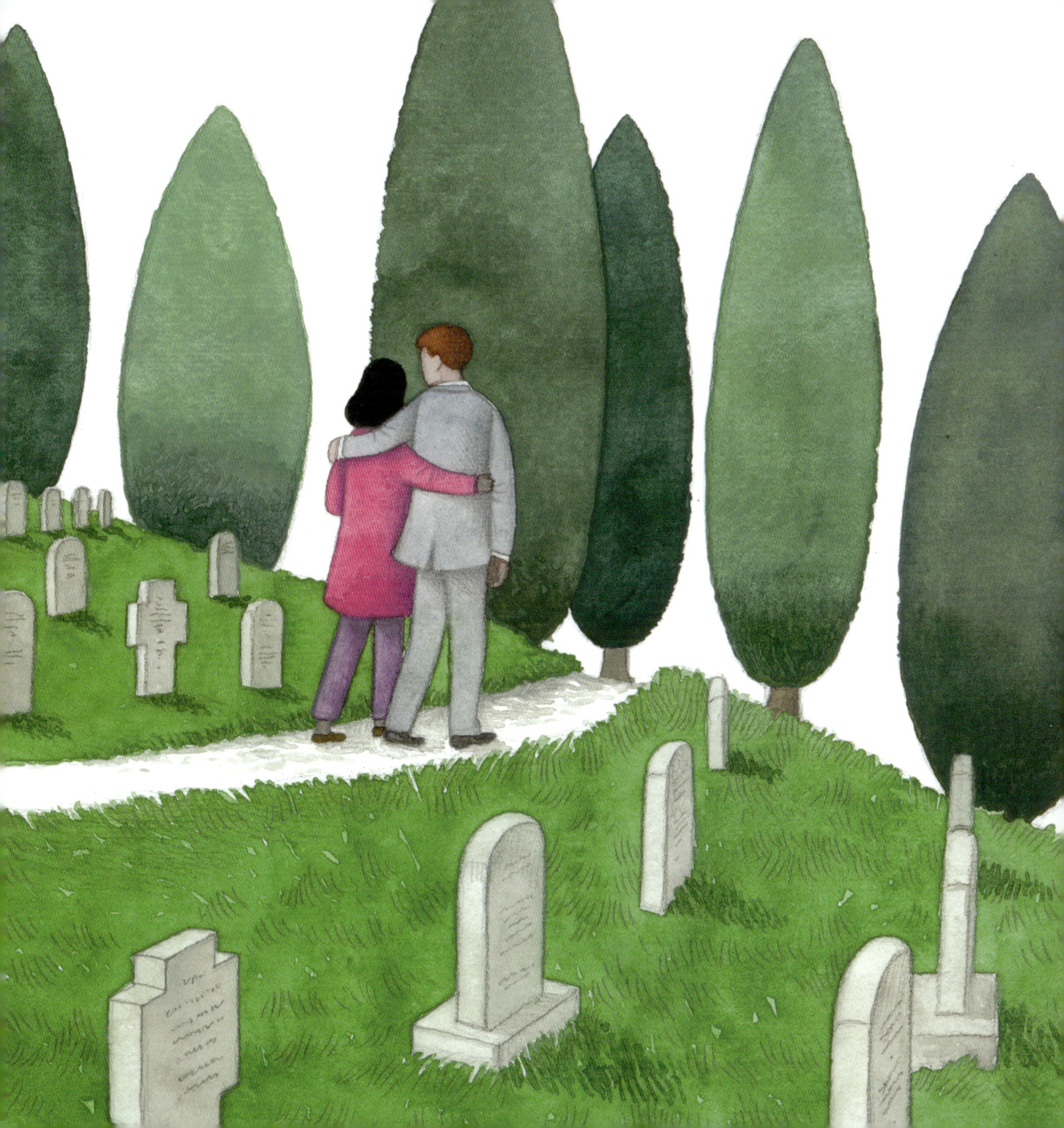

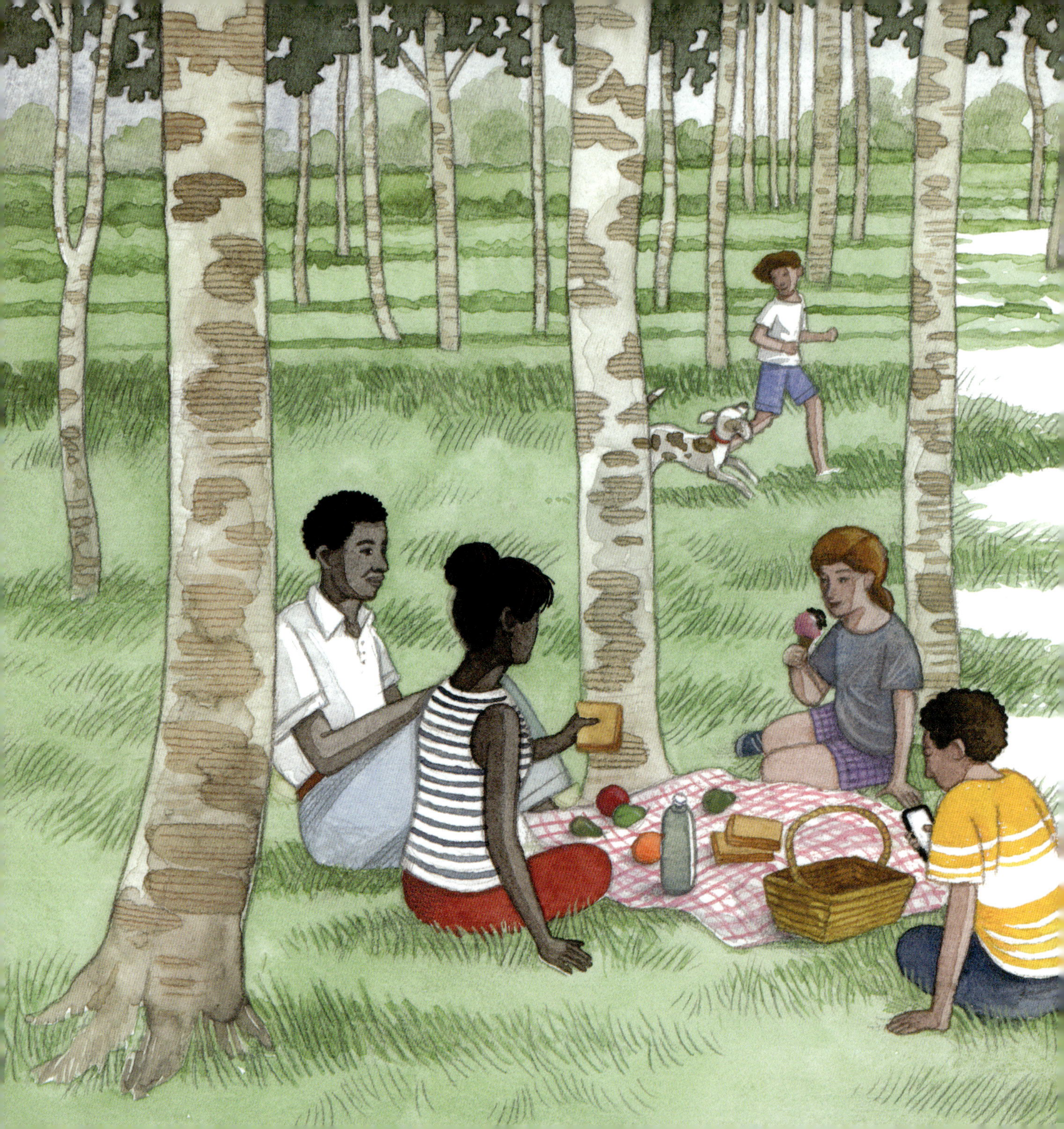

Some people think that all you need to get married is love. They say, "Love makes a marriage." Well, love is a big part of it! But there are a lot of things that people love—their pets, a beautiful sunset, ice cream sundaes—but no one marries those things!

Marriage is about love, but it's about more than love. Marriage is a vow, a sacred promise. When a man and a woman get married, they promise God that—no matter what—the man will stay with the woman and the woman with the man as long as they both live. A bride and groom make these promises because sometimes it is hard to love each other. Marriage vows help keep a couple together even when they don't feel like loving each other.

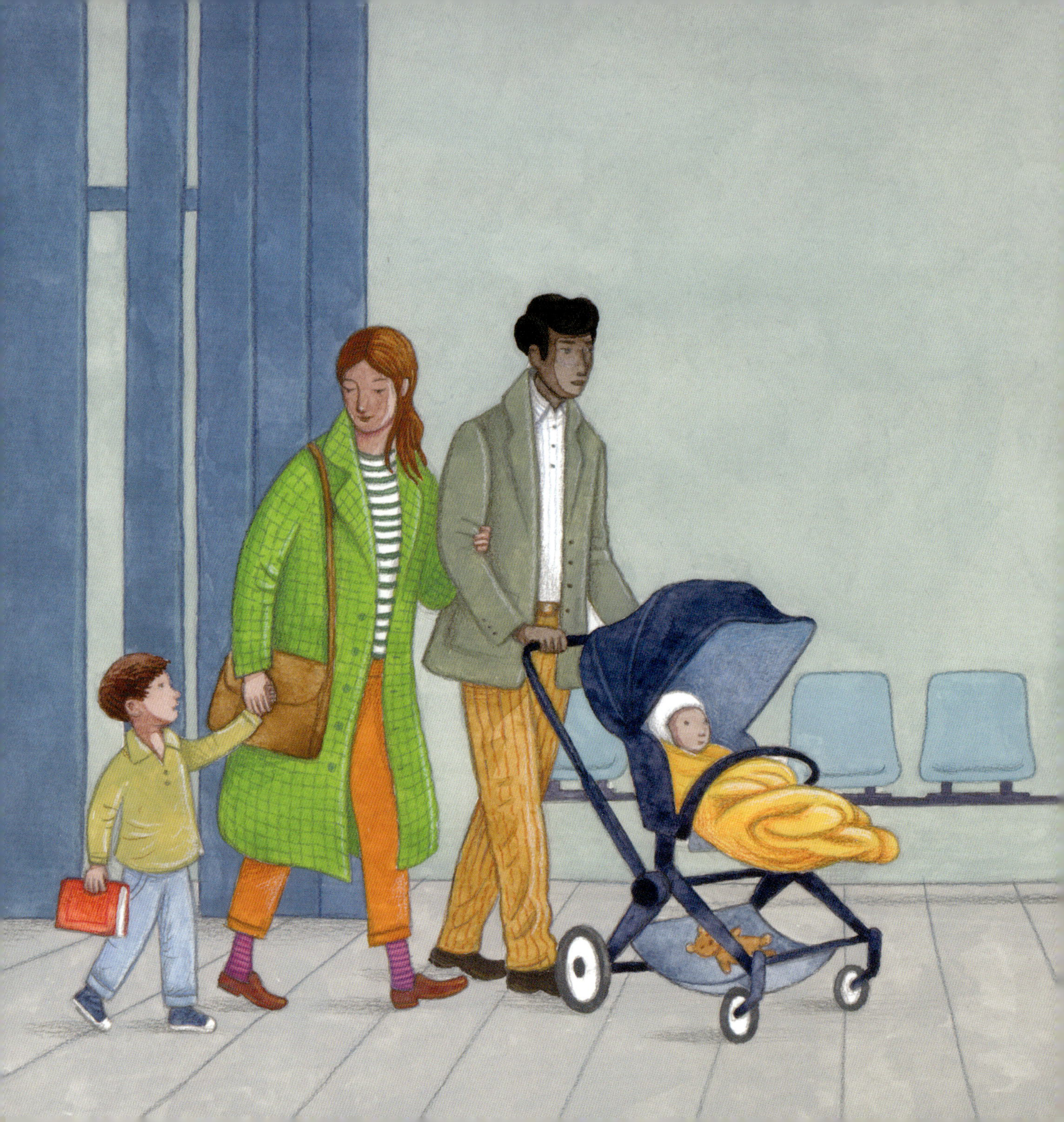

No matter what—the man will stay with the woman and the woman won't leave the man as long as they both live. Keeping married couples together is so good that most countries have laws about marriage. Most people know that marriage between one man and one woman for their whole life makes a country strong because it gives kids like you a safe place to grow up and become strong. Safe, loving families make healthy communities, and healthy communities around the world and in every culture make strong countries, and everyone wins!

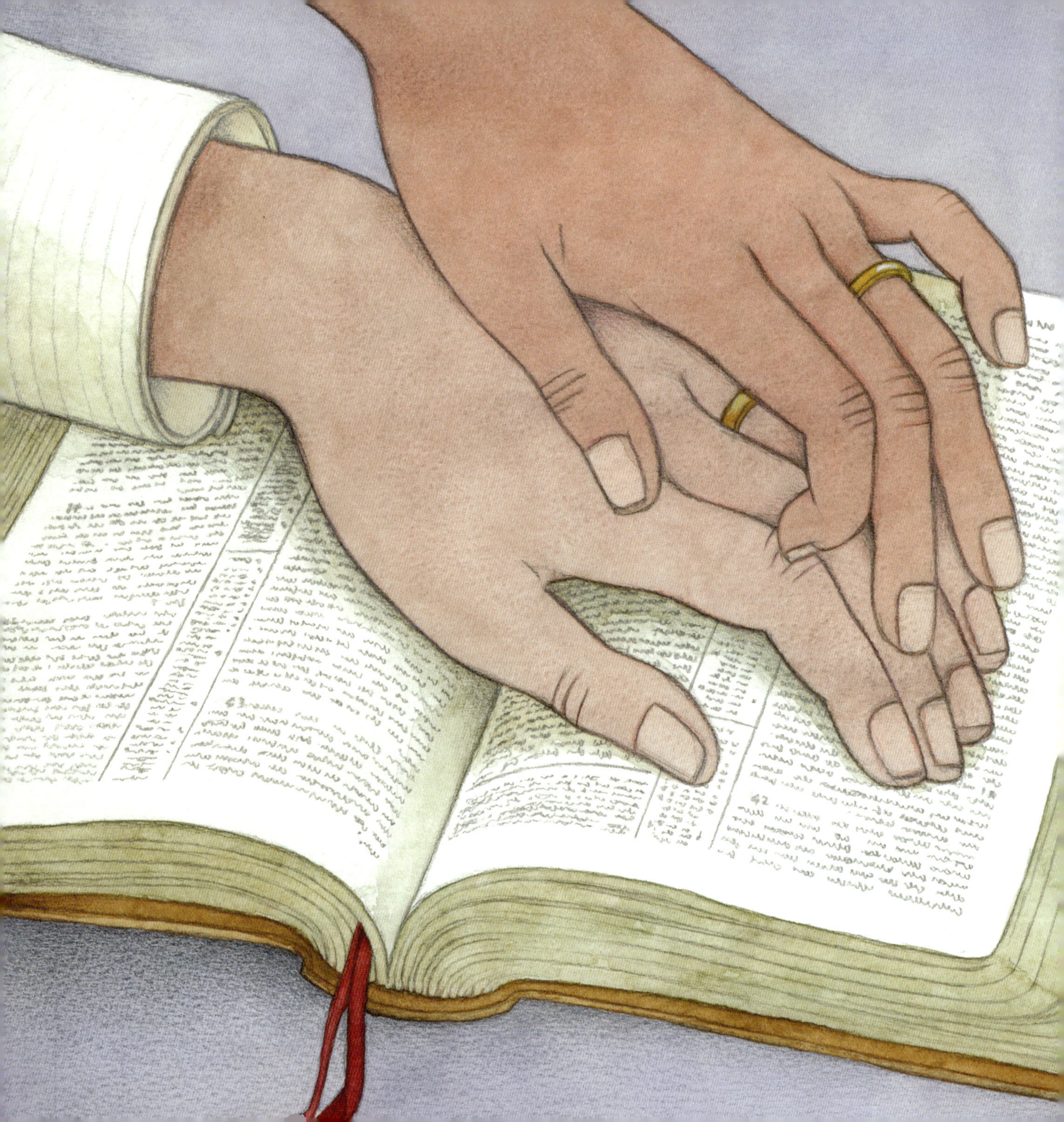

Not all countries or leaders agree on what marriage should be, but no matter what country you live in—and no matter what their laws about marriage are—don't get confused! There are laws of the land and there are God's laws, and they are not always the same.

What God says about marriage matters most. God's way is always loving, and His way is always best. God's Word, our Holy Bible, tells us that everyone is to respect and value marriage (Hebrews 13:4). That means we are to keep our marriage promises and help others keep their promises, too. We are not always good at keeping promises, though. Sometimes we're better at breaking our promises than we are at keeping them. God understands that we are promise-breakers—that we are broken and the world we live in is broken (Genesis 3:6-7).

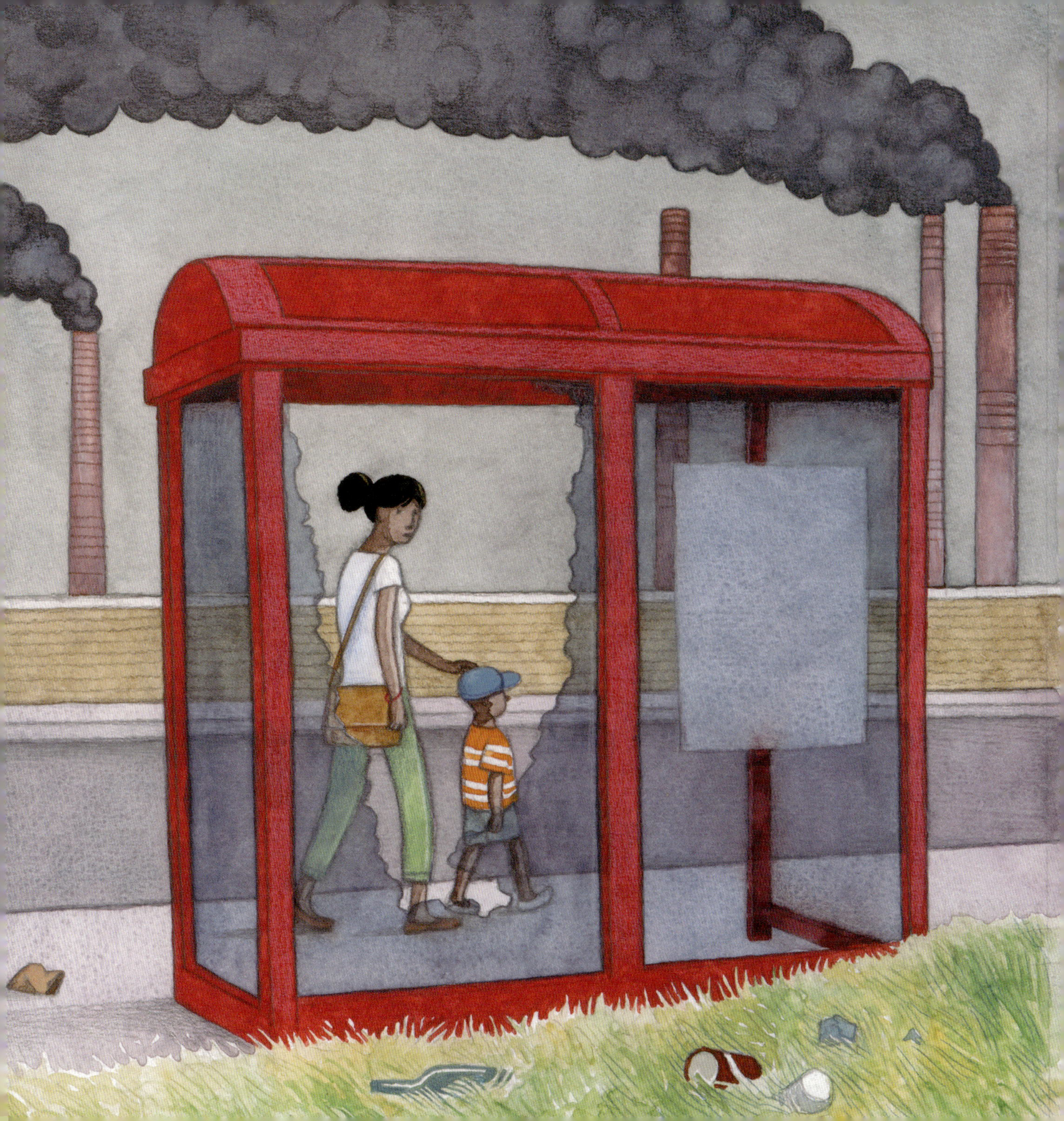

*S*ometimes grown-ups even break their marriage promises. Sadly, a marriage can turn ugly and painful. Sometimes sin can harden our hearts, and we hurt the ones we're supposed to love the very most.

If your parents are divorced, that hurts and God understands that pain. He promises to be near you when your heart is sad (Psalm 34:18), and help you when everything is so hard (Isaiah 41:10). You can talk to Him about it all.

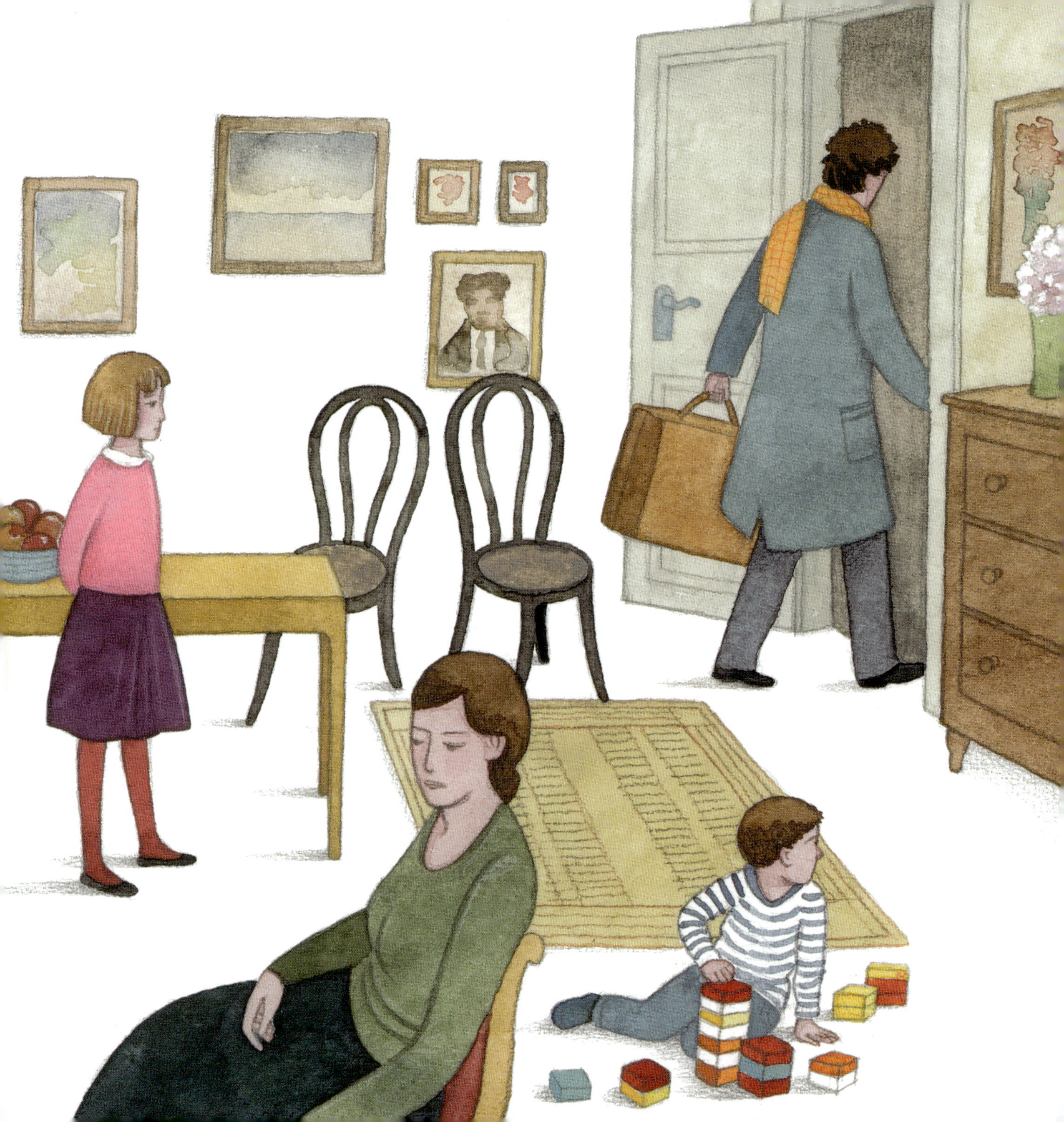

Some people get mixed up in another way. Some people think that marriage can be between two men or two women or that a husband can have more than one wife. Some people think everyone will be happier if they can do whatever they want and decide for themselves what marriage should be.

Sometimes we want the wrong things, things that we think will make us happy but really can't. God teaches us about true happiness. He says that real, forever happiness only comes from knowing and following Him (Psalm 62:1).

Part of following God is believing what He says about marriage. Marriage isn't what we think it should be. Marriage is what God says it should be. Why? Because God made us and God made marriage. God says marriage is between one man and one woman for life, and God's way is always loving and best.

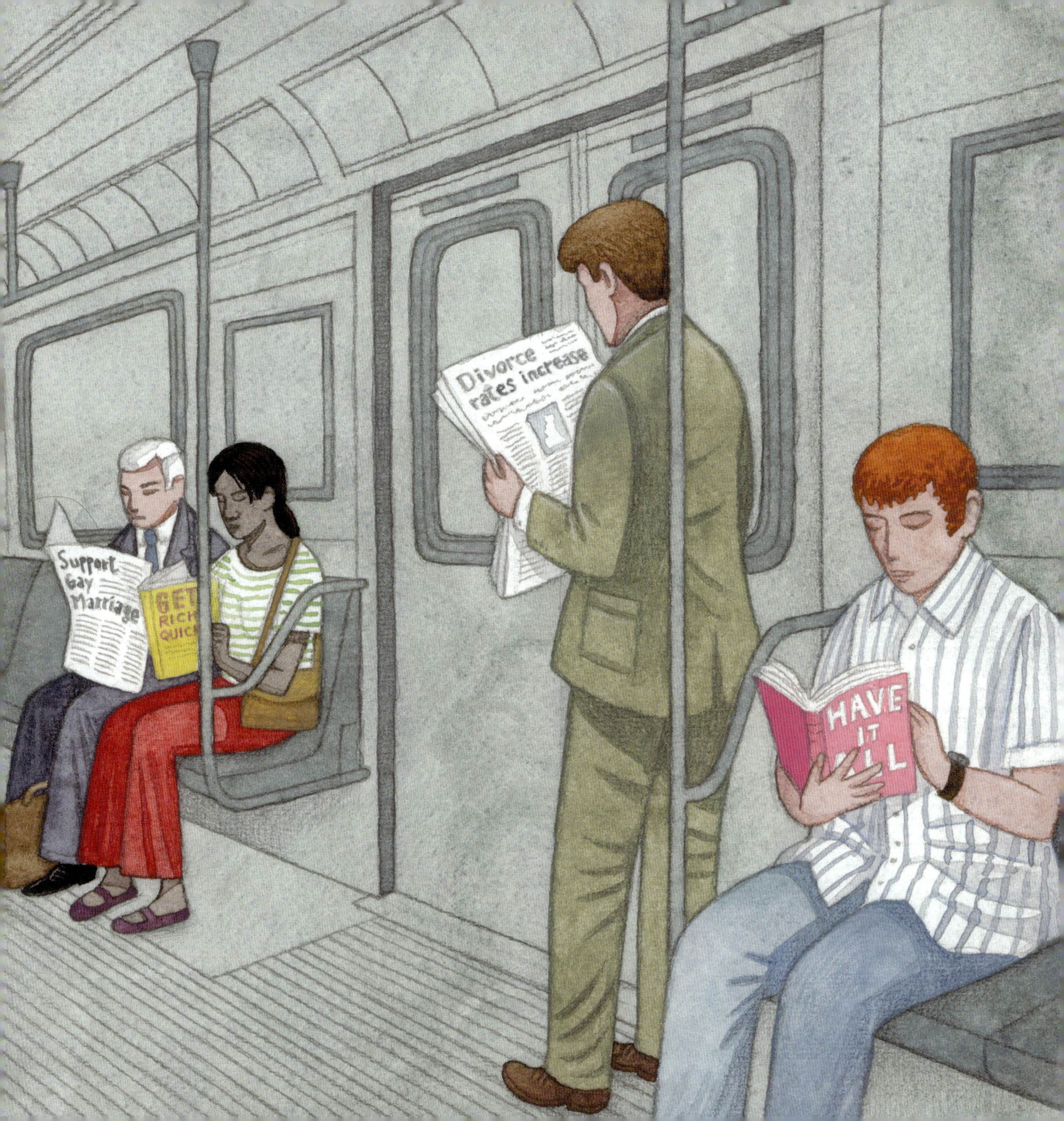
Support Gay Marriage
Divorce rates increase
HAVE IT

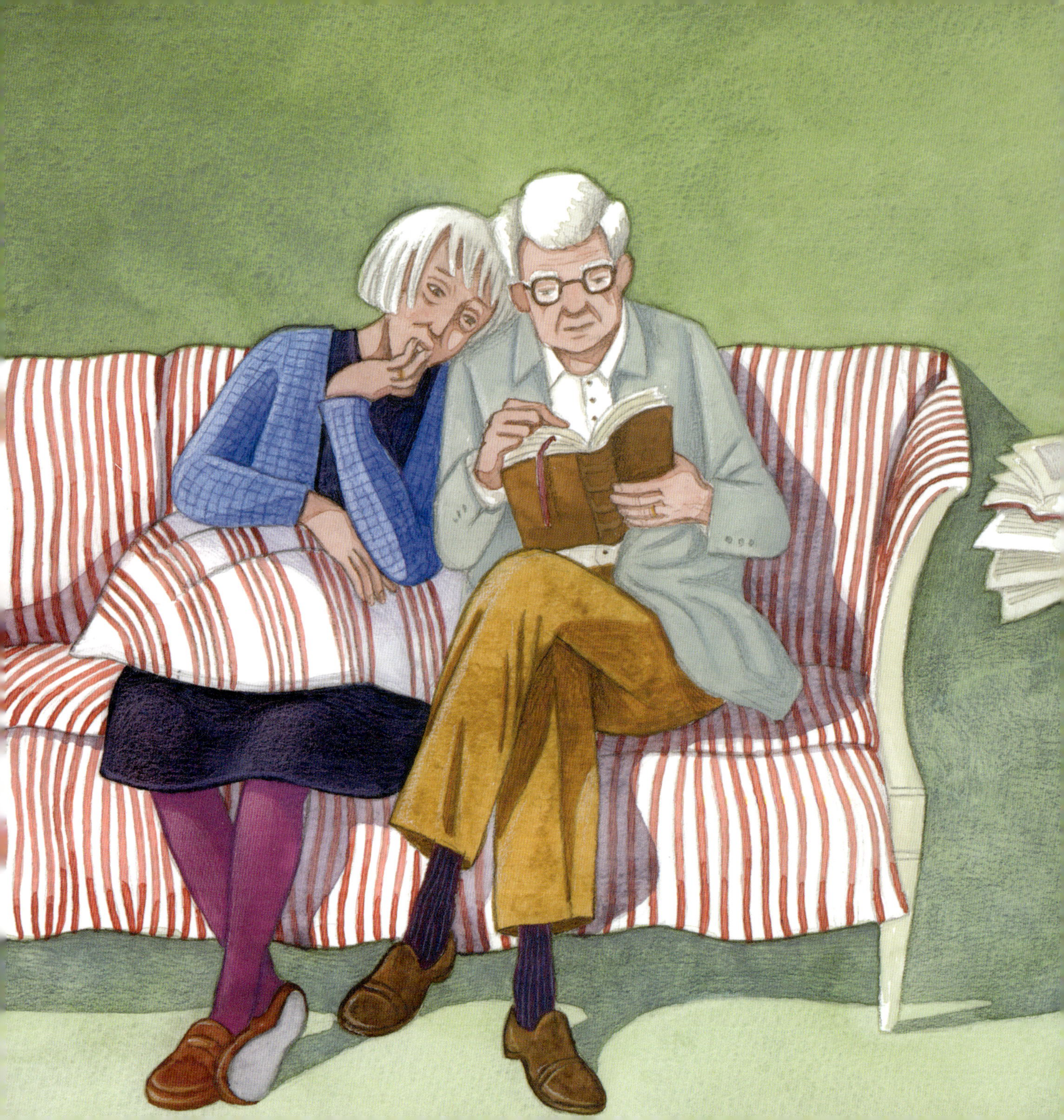

Do you know someone who doesn't believe what the Bible says about marriage—maybe someone in your neighborhood or someone in your family? You must never be unkind or say mean things about them. God wants you to be kind and loving, and God's way is always best (Zechariah 7:9, Titus 3:4-5).

Someday you may get married. It will be wonderful! Marriage will also be hard. It is difficult to be selfless when you live all the time, every day of your life, with another person. It is hard to put someone else ahead of yourself. But it is possible that a marriage could be the most loving, deep and happy relationship you will have with any other human being!

Be kind to
one another,
tenderhearted,
forgiving one
another, as God in
Christ forgave you.
Ephesians 4:32

A biblical marriage shows the world a tiny picture for all to see of the Big Romance—the one between Christ and His Church in love together. When you love Jesus, then you are a part of that Church and nothing and no one will ever be able to separate you from God's love for you (Romans 8:38-39).

How kind God is to give us marriage. Let's treat marriage with honor and thank God for this gift (Hebrews 13:4). Think of it! Marriage brings joy to grown-ups. Marriage is good for children. Marriage helps keep communities safe and countries strong.

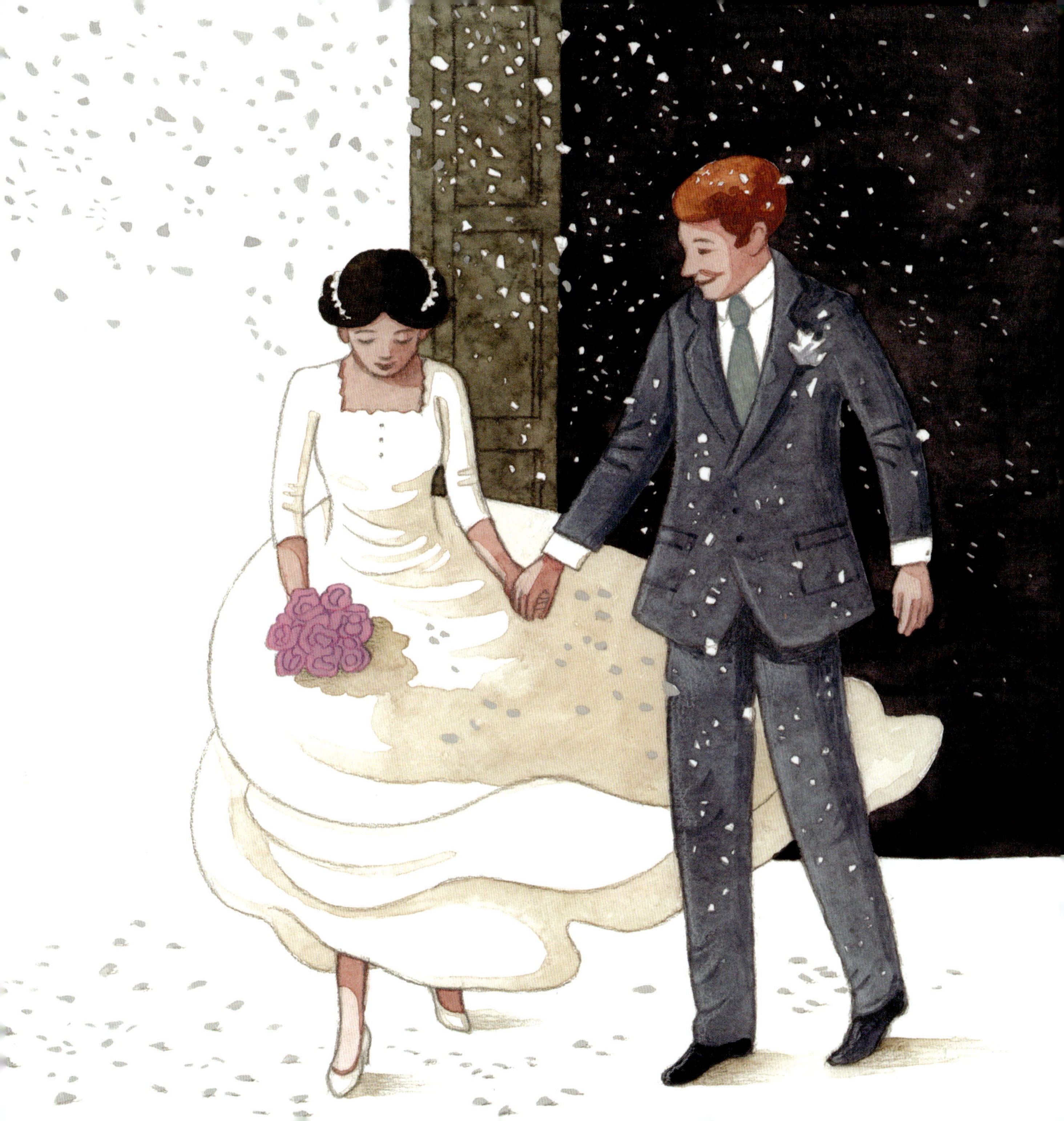

Best of all, marriage is an up-close display of the forever love of Jesus for His people.

God's way is always best!

Dear Heavenly Father,
thank you for your beautiful gift of
marriage!
Thank you for the Bible,
which teaches us about what
marriage
is and what it is not.
Thank you that all your ways
are loving and good
and that we can trust you with
everything—with our hearts
and our families
and our whole lives.
Please give us grace
to know and trust you more.
In Christ's name,
Amen.

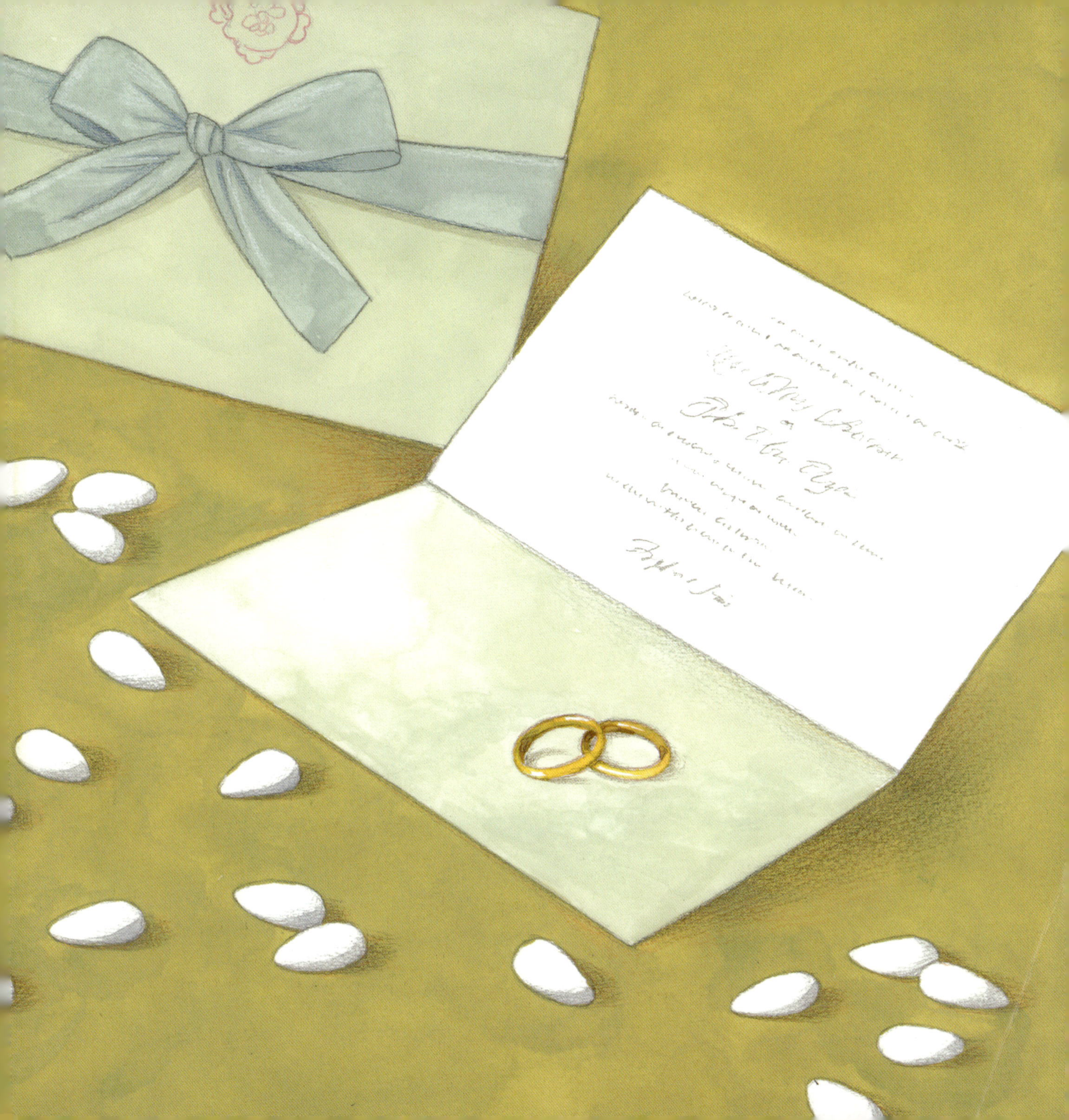

Dear Parent,

I hope you find this book to be a helpful tool as your little one grows in awareness of how families are formed. Children love to pretend to be grown-ups and do grown-up things. They see many different kinds of families with various parental arrangements, and this can be confusing to them.

Why not help children from a very early age take into their hearts what God teaches about marriage? Why not give young children a biblical vision of what, in God's kindness, could lie ahead for them?

Use this book during family devotions as you encounter biblical passages about marital love. Read it with your child when someone they know is about to be married. Give it to a young flower girl or ring-bearer. Share it together with your family as your wedding anniversary approaches and tell about the wonder of your own love story. Pray together for his or her future spouse.

However you choose to use this book, help build your child's love for—and trust in—his Heavenly Father. Show the little ones in your sphere of influence that you believe with all your heart that God's way is always best!

JANI ORTLUND

Christian Focus Publications

Christian Focus Publications publishes books for adults and children under its four main imprints: Christian Focus, CF4K, Mentor and Christian Heritage. Our books reflect our conviction that God's Word is reliable and Jesus is the way to know him, and live for ever with him. Our children's list includes a Sunday School curriculum that covers pre-school to early teens, and puzzle and activity books. We also publish personal and family devotional titles, biographies and inspirational stories that children will love. If you are looking for quality Bible teaching for children then we have an excellent range of Bible stories and age-specific theological books. From pre-school board books to teenage apologetics, we have it covered!

10 9 8 7 6 5 4

Copyright © 2018 Jani Ortlund

ISBN: 978-1-5271-0030-5

Published in 2018 and reprinted in 2021, 2022 and 2023 by Christian Focus Publications Ltd. Geanies House, Fearn, Tain, Ross-shire, IV20 1TW, Great Britain

Illustrations by Angelo Ruta

Cover Design: Tom Barnard

Printed in China

All rights reserved. No part of this publication may be reproduced, stored in a retrieval system, or transmitted, in any form, by any means, electronic, mechanical, photocopying, recording or otherwise without the prior permission of the publisher or a licence permitting restricted copying. In the U.K. such licences are issued by the Copyright Licensing Agency, 4 Battlebridge Lane, London, SE1 2HX. www.cla.co.uk
Scripture quotations are from The Holy Bible, English Standard Version, copyright © 2001 by Crossway Bibles, a division of Good News Publishers. Used by permission. All rights reserved. ESV Text Edition: 2007.